W9-BPN-085

Inventions That Shaped the World

MOTION PICTURES

R O B Y N   C O N L E Y

Franklin Watts
A Division of Scholastic Inc.
New York • Toronto • London • Auckland • Sydney
Mexico City • New Delhi • Hong Kong
Danbury, Connecticut

Photographs © 2004: Brown Brothers: 44 (Eadweard Muybridge), 23, 35; Classic PIO Partners: chapter openers; Corbis Images: cover left, 18, 29, 56, 57, 60, 61, 65, 66 (Bettmann), 50 (W.K.L. Dickson), cover right, 15 (Hulton-Deutsch Collection), 67 (James Leynse), 17, 64 (Royalty-Free), 16 (Sean Sexton Collection), 51; Culver Pictures: 6 (Prof. John Draper), 24, 26, 27, 30, 38, 46, 62; Edison National Historic Site/National Park Service, US Department of the Interior: 31 right, 31 left, 33, 42; Getty Images: 69 (Tim Boyle), 9 (Mark Wilson); Hulton|Archive/Getty Images: 19; J.T. Morrow: cover background, 48; Kobal Collection/Picture Desk: 58 (MGM), 54; Mary Evans Picture Library: 40; Nick Romanenko: 21 top, 37; Smithsonian Institution, Washington, DC/National Museum of American History, Electricity Collection: 39; Superstock, Inc.: 12; The Art Archive/Picture Desk: 7 (Dagli Orti/Musee des Beaux Arts Lyons); The Image Works: 20 (NMPFT/Bradford/HIP), 14, 21 bottom, 22 (NMPFT/Topham-HIP), 8 (Public Record Office/Topham-HIP), 13 (Science Museum, London/Topham-HIP).

Cover design by Kathleen Santini
Book production by Jeff Loppacker

Library of Congress Cataloging-in-Publication Data

Conley, Robyn.
    Motion pictures / Robyn Conley.
       p. cm. — (Inventions that shaped the world)
    Summary: Describes the invention of the motion picture, the impact it has had on modern culture, and the patterns of change that resulted from its discovery and use. Includes bibliographical references and index.
       ISBN 0-531-12332-4 (lib. bdg.)   0-531-16735-6 (pbk.)
    Cinematography—History—Juvenile literature. [1. Cinematography—History.] I. Title. II. Series.
          TR848.C66 2003
          778.5′3′09—dc22   2003015209

CONTENTS

CHAPTER ONE

CAMERAS CAPTURE THE WORLD

Do you enjoy watching movies at theaters and munching popcorn? Sometimes renting a video and stretching out on the couch with your family is fun to do on rainy weekends. You might discover what other countries are like if the movie was filmed in a land across the ocean. You might hear new languages spoken if a character in the video is from a culture different from yours. If you live in a warm climate and the movie features snowmobiles and ski resorts, you could imagine playing in the powdery white stuff.

People Share Themselves and Their World Through Photographs

What would it be like if you had only photographs to look at, with no moving pictures and no sound? Would you feel as connected to the images? If you had lived during the 1880s, you most likely wouldn't have seen moving pictures.

When cameras were first created, they could make photographs only. These grainy images were faint and sometimes blurry. Even so, any pictures developed during this time period were remarkable because they recorded faces and places that some people might never have seen in person. A photograph could travel in the mail across the country or across the world for far less money than a person could travel. Cousins who lived hundreds of miles apart could finally know what their relatives looked like. Someone with a camera in Egypt could take a picture of a pyramid and send it to a person in New York. Perhaps this idea of sharing each other's worlds helped with the invention of motion pictures. People were curious about other people in other parts of the world.

This photograph of Catherine Draper was taken in 1840 in New York City. Though the quality is poor, it is one of the earliest sunlit pictures of a human face.

6

A photograph could capture, in an instant, a moment in time that could be shared by many and that could surpass time.

Over time, better cameras that allowed people to take clearer pictures were invented. Stronger films that could bend and move were also invented. These new films could hold many pictures and could be wound through a **projector**. Projectors were machines that used light to project the pictures onto a screen so that more than one person at a time could see the continuous stream of photographs. Before long, entire rooms of people could see short films about places they might want to travel to. They could see

A filmed boxing match is shown to a full theater in this 1899 illustration. Projectors allowed groups of people to view events and places that they might not otherwise have been able to see.

news stories about events that happened all over the world. With one camera, a person could record actions in one community and share them with communities across nations.

People Keep a Watch on One Another

Today we can see weather disasters, news events, and sports competitions live from anywhere a satellite can project an image. Adults can learn job skills by watching training videos. Football players and other athletes often study reruns of their practices and games so that they can improve their abilities on the playing field. You might even rent a recording of your favorite band or singer to enjoy a "live" performance in your own family room.

From the early days of motion pictures, it was clear that the rolling images across the screen would change lives in ways few people had ever imagined. A hundred years ago, young people would never believe that families could use personal video or digital cameras to record weddings and

Today cameras are used not only for entertainment but also for surveillance. Here, police officers watch surveillance camera monitors in Washington, D.C.

birthdays. Sheriffs on horseback in the 1890s would be amazed at today's police cars that have video cameras mounted on their dashboards. And customers who shopped in rural general stores never had to pay for candy or apples under the watchful eye of a *surveillance camera* hung over the checkout counters.

People have always enjoyed watching films that are entertaining. Today they can also see pictures that help to record important moments, help to run their businesses more effectively, and help to keep their loved ones safe. With every new moving image, it seems, a new possibility for its use emerges. Motion pictures also have increased economic growth, bringing acting, sound recording, directing, and set-building jobs into a broader marketplace than live theater.

All these changes were brought about by imaginative thinkers and storytellers who began tinkering with moving pictures hundreds of years ago.

PICTURES, PROJECTORS, AND PRODUCTION COMPANIES

Before the existence of cameras or film, storytellers created the illusion of "moving pictures" by using drawings and light. Most of these storytellers used a device commonly called a *magic lantern* to show off their artwork. A magic lantern consisted of a boxlike case with a chimney through the top, a lens in front, and a burning candle and mirrors inside its walls. Colorful hand-painted drawings on glass slides passed through the box's middle. The lighted candle, combined with the lens, illuminated the image of the drawing, and the mirrors positioned inside reflected the much larger image onto a sheet or wall outside the lantern. The devices were clever in design and worked well for the time. Their popularity grew as illustrations became more complex and their use increased for both entertainment and education.

THE MAGIC LANTERN

Between 1644 and the early 1800s traveling storytellers often used devices called magic lanterns to illustrate their tales. Many of the stories included ghosts, goblins, and other elements of magic that were popular at the time, and that's why the boxes that lit up were called magic lanterns. Before long, magic lanterns were being used in schools and homes as learning tools and toys. There were small ones that children could operate, and large ones that were made of brass and had extra lenses. The larger lanterns projected images onto a screen so that many people could see the pictures at one time. Courtyards or large buildings where many people gathered to watch magic-lantern shows soon became known as theaters. Over time, music and other sound effects were added to the storytellers' words and pictures, making the lantern productions even more elaborate and entertaining.

Magic lanterns played a large part in Victorian society. Lectures on religion, education, and world events were relayed by photographic and hand-painted images. This is a hand-painted slide of Hekla Volcano in Iceland.

The **zoetrope** was invented in 1834 by William George Horner in England. It was **patented** in America in 1867. This round device featured pictures on glass inside a rotating

In the 1860s a popular viewing device used to create the effect of motion was the zoetrope. It paved the way for the development of the presentation of animated images.

drum that had slots in its side. People looked through the slots as they cranked the drum to watch the pictures moving in front of their eyes.

14

Film and Camera Troubles

In the late 1800s mechanical inventions entered the world in a major way. The telephone rang and the automobile rumbled into existence during the last two decades of the nineteenth century. Men with big ideas created machines that in turn helped other inventors' ideas to work better. This is how motion pictures developed.

The first cameras were invented at this time. Early cameras were bulky and shaped a little like a square telescope, with one wide end and one narrow end. A thin sheet of paper was pressed between glass plates inside the camera. The paper was coated with a liquid known as an *emulsion*, which consisted partly of silver nitrate. When the camera operator took a picture by opening the shutter of the camera and letting light in, the silver nitrate burned the image of what had been photographed onto the paper between the plates. Then the paper was removed and soaked in other chemicals, which

A nineteenth-century photographer at work

15

allowed a picture to develop on the paper.

Being a photographer took a lot of muscles. The cameras were heavy to move around, and so were all the chemicals, plates, and papers needed for developing the images. People needed smaller cameras and an easy-to-use **film** if photography were to become popular.

Taking pictures in the nineteenth century was not easy. A photographer had to carry his camera, as well as the chemicals, plates, and paper needed to develop the image.

Roll 'Em

Amateur photographer George Eastman did develop a simple film. Eastman had wanted to find a way to mold film into rolls instead of individual sheets. He hoped that pictures could be taken with one long piece of film, making the glass plates unnecessary, and developed later. After years of hard work, Eastman came up with a process that used strips of paper that were about the width of a ruler, but much longer. He coated the thin strips with a gelatin-and-chemical mixture to make a bendable surface. Then he applied another coat, made of a light-sensitive gelatin that contained chemicals to expose the pictures.

16

To develop the gelatin-based film, Eastman removed the paper backing and placed the film on a transparent sheet of gelatin. Then he transferred the layers of gelatin onto a treated paper that would permanently capture the image. Sometimes Eastman would varnish the transparent sheet of gelatin that contained the photographed image, creating a sturdy but bendable "rolled" film. With Eastman's success, it wasn't long before rolls of bendable film became a key step in making motion pictures.

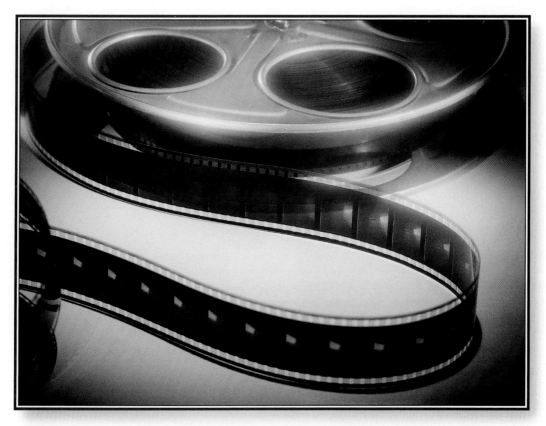

Bendable film changed photography by allowing for "moving" pictures.

GEORGE EASTMAN

George Eastman was born in 1854 in Waterville, New York. As an adult he was a banker with a passion for photography. When he started taking pictures, Eastman didn't like carrying around the glass plates and the tanks of emulsion chemicals that were needed because the pictures had to be developed right away. Then after he had developed them, he had to wait for them to dry before he could go on to another project. He was impatient with all the steps.

When Eastman read that British photographers used a gelatin emulsion surface instead of messy chemicals and plates, he started experimenting with formulas. After nearly three years he came up with a dry gelatin formula instead of the wet chemical formula he had been using.

When more and more photographers wanted to use his "dry plate process," Eastman developed a machine that could prepare a large number of these gelatin-based plates at a time. Before he knew it, his hobby had turned into a profitable business.

Cameras and Projectors

Two other inventions that emerged in the late 1880s also led to major improvements in making and viewing motion pictures. These devices, invented by Thomas Edison, were the **Kinetograph** and the **Kinetoscope**.

The Kinetograph was one of the first motion-picture cameras. It used a shutter device that opened and closed after each frame of film was shot. The film then moved forward on a sprocket system similar to how a bicycle chain moves on a gear. Later, when the film moved forward, the eye was fooled into believing that the images on the film had moved, but in reality

Thomas Edison's Kinetograph was the forerunner to the movie camera. Frame by frame, it captured still images that when viewed appeared to have moved. However, only the frames had moved.

only the frames of the film had moved. Each frame had a slightly different image on it. It was the speed of the moving frames that made the eye "see" movement.

To view the films that had been shot, people used a Kinetoscope. These viewers were boxlike cabinets with a peephole at the top that a person looked down into to see the pictures. The cabinets were coin-operated like today's arcade games and were delivered to places called parlors or theaters. People inserted nickels into the slots of Kinetoscopes so that they could watch the latest "moving pictures."

Although men and women of all ages enjoyed dropping their coins into the machines and seeing pictures move, there was a down side to the invention. Only one person could use a Kinetoscope at a time. To make motion pictures accessible to more people, a different viewing method was needed.

These images, filmed in 1895, show the effect of movement frame by frame.

People would wait in line to have the chance to view a film through a Kinetoscope.

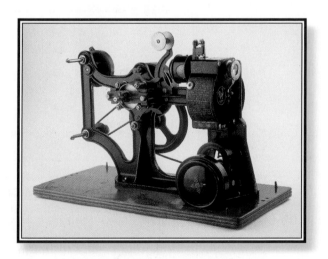

This projector made home movies a reality in 1912. Film wound around a reel, passing by a light that illuminated moving images onto a screen or a wall.

Soon another major invention—the projector—brought motion pictures to even larger audiences than the magic lanterns ever did. Projectors had wheel-shaped reels that ran the bendable film past a light source. This light source then projected the film's magnified image onto a screen. Now people no longer had to individually peek into a Kinetoscope to see pictures move. They could relax in comfortable chairs with family or friends and watch giant images on a flat white screen.

This ability to show motion pictures to larger audiences helped make the movie industry into the giant it is today.

THE LUMIÈRE BROTHERS

Auguste and Louis Lumière were brothers who lived in Lyons, France, during the late 1800s. Their father, Antoine, was a supplier of photographic equipment. One day in 1894 he traveled to Paris to watch a demonstration of Edison's Kinetoscope. The invention interested Antoine, and he bought a strip of the film to bring home to his sons, who worked for him. He wanted them to try to invent an inexpensive motion-picture machine that projected images onto a wide screen.

Both brothers loved working with scientific ideas, and each had a talent for technical devices. On February 13, 1895, the brothers patented their new invention, called a Cinématographe (right). Although this machine was a camera, a printer, and a projector all in one, it weighed much less than Edison's Kinetoscope. More important, the Cinématographe projected the images onto a screen so that many people could view the same motion picture at a time.

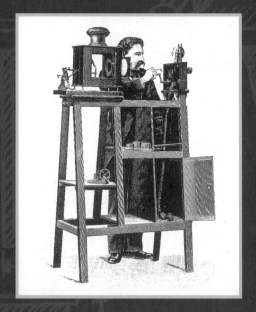

The family held a screening of their first motion picture using the Cinématographe on March 22, 1895. The audience loved the new invention! Louis made many actuality films—films of real events—and the Lumières started opening theaters to show their pictures. They called these places *cinémas*, short for Cinématographe, a word still used today in many theater names.

People Want More Moving Pictures

With the advancements in film, cameras, and projectors, many great changes took place in the motion-picture process. The quality of the pictures improved, and people everywhere wanted to watch these new "moving pictures."

As the movie industry grew, the need for industry workers increased. Here a crew prepares a set for filming.

Before long, an industry formed that consisted of many people involved in making motion pictures, including actors, writers, directors, camera operators, lighting specialists, set designers, costume makers, and producers.

Buildings were needed to keep the actors and the motion-picture crews out of the weather for indoor scenes. Soon **studios** were constructed along the East Coast of the United

Indoor scenes of motion pictures were filmed in studios. They consisted of large open buildings that allowed as much sunlight in as possible for filming.

States. A studio was usually a large building or group of buildings. These places had lots of windows and sometimes even ceilings that opened to allow as much sunlight in as possible. The inside portion of the studios had few walls, so big sets could be built and actors could move around easily.

Edison's First Film Studio

One of the first studios in America opened in New Jersey in February 1893, under the leadership of inventor Thomas Edison. Edison and his employees had already perfected much of the design on Kinetographs and Kinetoscopes when they started work on a studio that could pivot and move. This design used tracks and people power to move the building. The frame of the building was built on rail wheels, much like a train's wheels, to ride on tracks. When the studio needed to be moved, the movie crew pushed the building along the tracks. This allowed the motion-picture crews to use the best light of the day—all day long. More light meant fewer shadows, making the films appear more crisp and clear to viewers. Another interesting addition to Edison's studio was the movable ceiling that could be opened to allow even more sunlight in if it were needed.

Because Edison's first motion-picture camera was huge and as heavy as a grand piano, all films had to be shot inside the studio. Some of the early stars of motion pictures were

BLACK MARIA

Workers who built Thomas Edison's studio called it the Black Maria. They thought the boxy building was ugly. It was two stories tall and totally covered in black tar paper. The building reminded the workers of the New Jersey police patrol wagons, which were called Black Marias. Edison's Black Maria did have something in common with the patrol wagons: It was mobile. The building's frame had built-in wheels that were placed in a track so that the whole thing could be moved with the sun. Its ceiling and roof also moved and could be opened to allow in more sunlight. The Black Maria may have been ugly, but the mobility and light that Edison desired for making motion pictures are still important elements in studio construction. Today a motion-picture studio costs millions of dollars to build, but the Black Maria cost only $637.67, a good sum in 1893.

Fred Ott worked for Thomas Edison in 1894. His sneeze became famous, for it was the subject for one of Edison's first copyrighted, still surviving films. It was filmed by W.K.L. Dickson, Edison's assistant.

not actors but simply the men and women who worked in Edison's lab. Most of these films lasted only twenty seconds and showed everyday happenings such as a man sneezing. Edison later brought performers to his studio to create longer and more-entertaining movies. Jugglers and dancers did their routines, boxers and wrestlers fought a few rounds, and magicians performed tricks in front of Edison's massive camera. Later those same people could watch their own performances at the neighborhood nickelodeon, another name for early movie theaters, because they usually charged five cents for admission.

A New Industry

When cameras became smaller and more mobile, lots of people wanted to learn how to make motion pictures. Before long, additional studios sprang up, started by people who had an interest in the art of moving images and telling stories. Most early films were called actualities. They featured famous people or news events such as disasters.

The popularity of the films surprised Edison, who believed that only children would be interested in motion pictures and that they would soon lose interest in them, as children often did in new things.

By 1900, however, motion pictures had created an industry. Actors were hired to appear in the films and directors to guide the actors. Construction crews helped build indoor and outdoor sets. Photography experts were needed to help movie directors learn about the best camera techniques and proper lighting. What had been tinkering in workshops became a major industry.

CHAPTER THREE

VIEWING THE INVENTOR

During the 1800s a great many people helped to invent moving pictures. Thomas Edison and his assistants, however, were the first Americans to build a workable camera and projector and then use them to make movies for the general public. Because Edison had so many ideas and inventors in his laboratory, some historians have wondered how much he personally helped with the development of motion pictures. His handwritten notes and drawings

I never perfected an invention that I did not think about in terms of the service it might give others. . . . I find out what the world needs, then I proceed to invent.

　　　　　　　—Thomas Alva Edison

29

during many stages of the motion picture's invention show he was as greatly involved with it as he was with his other ideas. Perhaps it was his ever-curious mind that allowed him to work on so many inventions at one time.

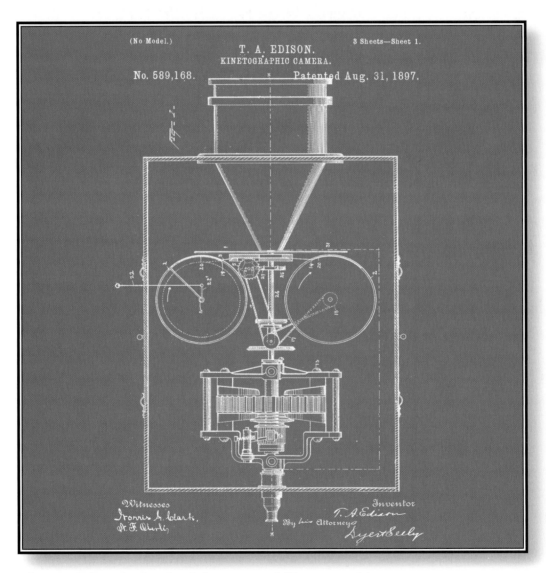

Thomas Edison's sketch of the patented Kinetographic camera

An Early Curiosity

Thomas Alva Edison was born on February 11, 1847, in Milan, Ohio. His parents were Sam and Nancy Edison, who already had six children. Edison's mother first thought the round-faced, fair-haired boy with such a large head might have had "brain fever." Later, as the baby grew, she learned that what her son really had was a huge curiosity.

By the time young Thomas, usually called Al by his family, was six years old, he had often wandered into trouble by

Thomas Edison said his mother, Nancy, "was the making of me . . . and someone I must not disappoint." His father, Sam, urged him to read the great classics, paying him ten cents for each one completed.

By the time Edison turned ten, he had built a crude lab in a corner of his family's cellar. This area was given to him after his mother scolded her son about the spilled chemicals and wet-cell battery mess he kept in his bedroom. She allowed him to spend a great deal of time down in the earthen cellar, where he experimented with the sciences that he loved and where it was safe to make a mess!

investigating how things worked. Once he burned down his family's barn because he wanted "to see what the flames would do." Another time, after asking his mother why hens sat on their eggs, the family found him sleeping in the chicken coop, warming the eggs so that they'd hatch as his mother had told him.

When he was still young, Edison's family moved to Port Huron, Michigan, where the extreme cold kept the boy in poor health. He couldn't even attend school until he was eight years old. By then he had no patience for sitting at a desk all day. But Edison's mother was sure he was bright, so she decided to teach him at home. She had taught other children at a small Canadian school before she had married. Her insight proved true. Under his mother's lively teaching style, Thomas Edison discovered a love for learning—and experimenting.

As an adult, Edison looked back on this time and said, "My mother was the making of me. She understood me; she let me follow my bent." His bent, however, did not include spending a lot of time with other kids. This concerned his father, who once said, "He spent the greater part of his time in the cellar. He did not share to any extent the sports of his neighborhood. He never knew a real boyhood like other boys."

A Real-World Education

Edison tried going back to school when he was eleven, but he had a difficult time paying attention. His curious mind wandered, which usually caused more problems. After only a year, he again gave up on school and took a job selling newspapers and snacks on the Grand Trunk Railway. This train carried people who lived in Port Huron to and from Detroit each day for work.

While working on the train, Edison gained another kind of education. He learned about common sense and how to work hard to succeed. He also became fascinated with the ***telegraph system***. The telegraph was the only method of communication between train depots.

Edison at around age eleven

YOUNG BUSINESSMAN

When Thomas Edison was fifteen and still working for the Grand Trunk Railway, the Civil War was raging across America. While in Detroit, he heard news about the horrible battle of Shiloh in Tennessee. He knew that story would sell lots of newspapers. Before his train left Detroit that evening to head back to Port Huron, he ordered more than a thousand newspapers to be placed on the train.

Edison sent word about the battle through the telegraph system to all the railway stations along the way. As he hoped, the papers sold fast at the stations. He even raised the price from one nickel to one quarter to make a bigger profit. Later in life Edison became as well known for his successful business practices as for his successful experiments. With his inventions such as the light bulb and the phonograph, he showed the world that they could be manufactured in mass quantities and sold for a solid profit.

During the 1850s and 1860s hardworking men strung telegraph wires all across America. They braved Indians, thunderstorms, and blizzards to connect people in cities through a language of electric dots and dashes. Edison's mind started whirling, and he decided to make his own telegraph. Working on his days off, Edison took wire that was usually used for suspending stovepipes and hung it between two buildings on his parents' land. He used glass bottles as *insulators* to keep the electric current

Long-distance communication became possible with the telegraph system. Electronic currents traveled through wires that activated an electromagnet that produced written codes on strips of paper.

from scorching the wood on the buildings. It was a rough design, but Edison's first telegraph worked. Its success inspired even more ideas and greater experiments.

A New Job, a New Invention

A major influence on the teenage Edison was James MacKenzie, a telegrapher who worked at the train station in Mount Clemons, Michigan. When the Grand Trunk Railway stopped each day in Mount Clemons, Edison left the train to learn more about telegraphy from MacKenzie. He even hired another boy to take over his train duties during his absence. After a few months, Edison became good enough at working the telegraph devices to become an operator for other stations and give up working on the train.

Edison's work habits were not great, because his mind wandered, just as it had when he tried to concentrate in school. This daydreaming caused him to overlook details, and he was often fired from the telegraph jobs, but it also helped him come up with the idea for his first practical invention.

Daydreaming Brings New Ideas

A mechanical device called a Morse register had been invented at this time. It was attached to the receiving end of a telegraph and used an electrically powered pointer to automatically punch Morse code dots and dashes into a thin strip of moving paper. This invention allowed the telegraphers to decipher the code into written messages any time after the Morse register received them.

Edison wondered if a repeating register that automatically copied these messages could be built. He later said, "I got two old Morse registers and arranged them in such a way that by running a strip of paper through them, the dots and dashes were recorded on it by the first instrument as fast as they were delivered."

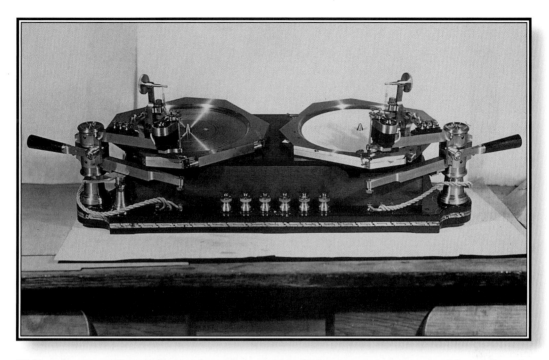

Edison's repeating telegraph register recorded messages on one side and automatically transmitted them through the other.

This repeating telegraph register was helpful because messages traveling long distances no longer had to be rekeyed from station to station. Following this success, the Western Union Telegraph Company wanted the inventive young man to try his hand at building a **duplex telegraph**. A duplex telegraph could send two messages at a time, doubling the number of messages Western Union could send and receive, which would also double its income.

In 1868 an article appeared in *The Telegrapher*, a news journal for people who worked in telegraphy. The news story detailed Edison's success with the duplex telegraph. It was just the boost of confidence Edison needed to devote all his time and energy to his inventions.

On His Own in a Team Setting

When Edison made enough money with the telegraphic machines, he could finally work solely on his own inventions in his own shop. His approach to inventing was different from other people's in that he hired a great many people with a variety of skills to tackle his ideas. Some

Edison's "invention factory" employed more than two hundred people with various skills to build products for a new and changing world.

people at the time called Edison's building, located in Menlo Park, New Jersey, the "invention factory."

One of his main associates was Charles Batchelor, an Englishman with whom Edison worked for decades. Together with others on Edison's team, they invented practical devices that made a big impact on how people lived. One of the best known was Edison's favorite: the phonograph. It later became known as the record player, which helped bring on the idea for today's

Charles Batchelor was one of Edison's closest assistants. He helped develop technologies such as telegraphy, electrical lighting, and the phonograph.

compact discs. The phonograph allowed people who might never go to a live concert to hear a popular singer's performance.

Edison's devotion to the phonograph eventually combined with his interest in making movies. During 1894 and 1895 Edison and his assistant, William Kennedy Laurie (W.K.L.) Dickson, began experiments in recording music and voices. They hoped to play these recordings along with motion-picture projection. By the end of 1895 he and

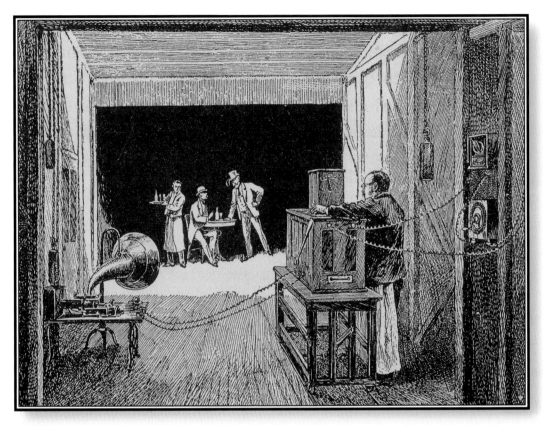

Edison's Kinetophone linked photographic impressions with sound recordings.

Dickson invented a **Kinetophone**. It was the first machine to connect sound with moving images.

Thomas Edison's interest in motion-picture technical advancements did not grow much after he perfected the Kinetophone. Instead he spent a great deal of time bringing lawsuits against other inventors and motion-picture makers. Edison failed to submit timely patents and often ended up taking people to court. He believed these people did not have a right to use the technology that his staff had developed.

Although many of the machines that other filmmakers used varied from Edison's designs, he still tried to stifle any motion-picture competition. Eventually his interest in the industry subsided completely.

Other major inventions by Edison and his team were incandescent lights, the first light bulbs, and a quality concrete. From 1870 through the mid-1920s, Edison and his workers also developed improvements in other products and set up businesses that successfully brought those products to the public.

INVENTION IMPROVEMENTS

One product improvement that Edison made was to the telephone designed by Alexander Graham Bell. Bell's device used a flexible membrane—made of rubber—that picked up the vibrations of a speaker's voice. These membranes did not provide the best reproduction of sound. Edison came up with the idea of using a carbon disk to replace the rubber membrane. The carbon disk made the reproduction of sound vibrations much more distinct.

An interesting twist to this story is that Alexander Bell's company came up with an improvement on Edison's phonograph. Edison's design used a tinfoil roller with raised spots that plucked reeds as the roller passed them. The plucked reeds then reproduced whatever sound had been recorded. The trouble with this design was that the tinfoil wore out after a certain amount of use. Bell came up with a wax cylinder that lasted much longer.

Thomas Edison married Mary Stilwell in 1871, and they had three children. After Mary died at age twenty-nine, he married Mina Miller, who also gave him three children. Edison had a habit of working long hours, even all night long sometimes.

It was obvious that Edison was more devoted to his work than to spending time with his family. Perhaps this is why they never worried when they saw him napping on a workbench or staying up all night. His hard work paid off in major ways. By

Thomas Edison taught his wife, Mina, Morse code. They would send one another private messages this way.

the time of his death on October 18, 1931, Thomas Edison had filed hundreds of patents and made living easier and more enjoyable for millions of people due to his curious mind and solid business sense.

CHAPTER FOUR

REELS OF MOTION, ACTION, AND HARD WORK

Have you ever had your picture taken and felt as if the camera's flash had blinded you? Most people say they can still see the flash long after the picture-taking session is over. Or maybe you've looked at a video game or a cloud formation for a long time and then blinked or glanced away from that image. Did the picture still stay on your mind's eye? This odd sensation, defined by Peter Roget in 1824, is called persistence of vision, and it was the basis for the first moving-picture system.

Persistence of Vision

Edison described persistence of vision this way: "The science is based upon what might be termed . . . a fraility or defect, in the human eye. The eye does not lose sight of an object the instant vision is intercepted. If I should place before your eye a photograph and then instantly shut off the range of sight, the impression of that photograph upon the retina of your eye and upon your brain would still remain for just a fraction of a second."

The man who best took advantage of this concept was a photographer named Eadweard Muybridge, who was known

Eadweard Muybridge photographed these images showing animal locomotion through sequential photography.

for his *sequential photography*. Sequential photography is the science of taking pictures in a sequence of a subject as it moves. In 1878, Muybridge set up an experiment at the Palo Alto Race Course in California to test this theory of persistence of vision and to try to capture "movement in film." He laid several trip wires that were connected to cameras a few feet apart. The wires were triggered when the horse ran past them, causing the cameras to take pictures of the animal in motion. When the pictures were developed and viewed in the sequence they were taken, they showed a cycle of the horse's movements. But the pictures were not one fluid motion.

Making "Motion"

Muybridge took his ideas about using multiple camera shots to make "moving" pictures to Thomas Edison in 1888. Edison combined Muybridge's work with his own knowledge about persistence of vision and encouraged his team to put their creative energies into building a camera that copied what our eyes did naturally.

A camera's lens opens and closes using a shutter. The shutter opens, snaps a picture by letting light in, then closes, imprinting an image on the film. One problem Edison's team faced was the film available at that time. It was thick and bulky and not easy to work with. When George Eastman invented a celluloid film that could be molded into long thin strips,

SEQUENCE PHOTOGRAPHER

Eadweard Muybridge was born in 1830 in Kingston on Thames, England. When he was in his twenties, he moved to the United States to take pictures of landscapes. The governor of California, Leland Stanford, asked him to photograph racehorses to analyze their movements. Stanford wanted to prove that when a horse was running full force all four of its hooves were off the ground at one time. Muybridge's photography helped prove Stanford right.

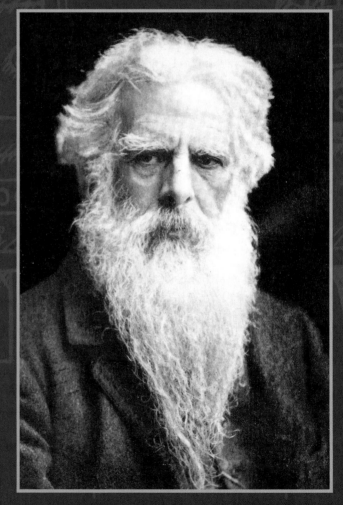

Muybridge also invented a process that used glass disks with several photographs on them. When a disk was spun in front of a magic-lantern lens, the images projected onto a screen seemed to move. He called the device a *zoopraxiscope*. It was one of the first devices that used photographed images in this way.

Edison knew it was perfect for his plan to make a system using a camera and a projector. Edison wanted to make all the pictures on a filmstrip pass in front of one lens, so that the pictures could be viewed through one peephole. The flexible filmstrip made this possible. A hand crank was attached to gears that moved the film so that people cranking the machine could view the film as quickly or as slowly as they desired.

The film had black spaces between each picture, or frame. When a filmstrip moved through the hand-cranked projector, the eyes saw "movement," even though each frame was a single picture separated by a black space. The brain stayed focused on the previous picture, and when the next picture passed in front of the eyes, they saw the new picture while remembering the previous picture. In other words, the "movement" was only an illusion created by the speed at which each picture passed before the eyes. The eyes' ability to "see" the same picture even after they had quit focusing on it helped make the illusion seem real.

Equipped finally with the long, thin strips of film, Edison's team, now located in West Orange, New Jersey, perfected the Kinetograph camera, which had a shutter that opened and closed automatically, and the Kinetoscope projector, which also had a shutter that opened and closed automatically. This allowed light to project the image in front of a lens onto a screen. Patents for these machines were filed on August 24, 1891.

KINETOSCOPE

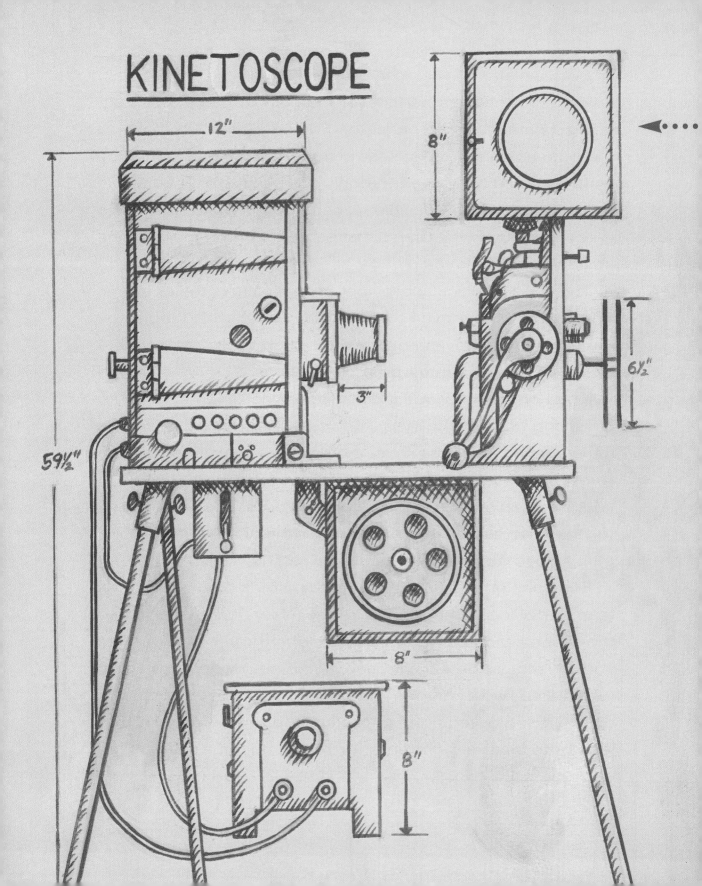

The first Edison Kinetoscopes were large boxlike cabinets that held many spools for a long, winding strip of film. Only one person at a time could view the images projected inside the box. They did this by cranking a handle that rotated the loop of film and turned the shutter wheel.

Edison's team of inventors worked hard to reduce the size of the machine. By 1902 there was only one loop of film between two reels, and it was operated electrically. They also created a projector that shot the images onto a large screen. All these improvements meant that the machine could be made for less money and that more people could watch the motion picture at one time.

Simple Changes Make Big Differences

Right away Edison's assistants tried to improve on both machines because they were huge and bulky and practical only for taking pictures of something that was right in front of the large camera. Also, only one person at a time could view the films from a Kinetoscope, limiting the number of people able to see each film. Edison, however, thought he could make more money charging each person to view a film separately, so he resisted the idea of a larger projection system.

A man who was important to the continued progress of motion pictures during 1888 was Edison's assistant, W.K.L. Dickson. Dickson's fascination with creating moving pictures kept Edison enthused, even when the great inventor wanted to move on to other projects once the Kinetograph and the Kinetoscope were making him money.

EDISON'S APPRENTICE

William Kennedy Laurie Dickson was born in 1860, in the town of Minihic-sur-Ranse, France. As a teenager, Dickson was interested in photography and in learning about any new method that could make pictures move. When he was nineteen, his family moved to London, where Dickson read stories in the newspapers about Edison's amazing laboratory. He wrote to Thomas Edison, asking to become an *apprentice* to the famous inventor. An apprentice is a person who studies another person's art or trade while working with him. At first Edison turned down the young man, but four years later, when Dickson's family moved to the United States, Edison hired Dickson to work at his West Orange facility.

Although Dickson worked hard for Edison, he eventually wanted to move out on his own to guarantee that all the patents to his inventions would remain in his name. Edison's company wanted all copyrights patented in Edison's name. He resigned from the company on April 2, 1895, and went to work designing a hand-held camera with some engineer friends he had met earlier. They succeeded in building, patenting, and selling the Biograph camera and the Mutoscope projector. The men officially went into business together, and Dickson returned to England as the manager of the Mutoscope and Biograph Syndicate's London office.

Most historians agree that if Dickson had not worked for Edison, Edison would never have continued to improve the camera and projection system. It was W.K.L Dickson who had the idea of punching holes on each side of the filmstrip so that those holes could fit over gear sprockets to move the film easily through the camera and the projector.

Of the invention of the motion-picture camera, Edison stated, "I am experimenting upon an instrument which does for the eye what the phonograph does for the ear, which is the recording and reproduction of things in motion."

Dickson also used recorded sound to play at the same time as a movie film was projected. He had a demonstration ready for Edison when the inventor returned from a trip to Europe. Edison was impressed, which enabled them to keep improving their camera and projection system. Dickson and other members of Edison's inventing team sometimes performed in the first movies. They acted out sneezing and dancing and other exaggerated actions that were easy to understand without sound.

The first simple films lasted less than twenty seconds, but as the newer machines took shape, the length and the quality of the film content also improved. Soon Edison had competition.

CHAPTER FIVE

PROGRESS, PROBLEMS, AND MORE POPULARITY

Edison had to keep improving his camera and projector system to stay competitive with others who had made their own cameras and projectors based on his original designs. When he couldn't compete with another device that might be better, he would purchase the company that produced it. This happened in 1895, when Edison's company bought Thomas Armat's Phantascope. The machine made by that company was an improved projector that showed movies on a large screen. Wealthy people began buying the projector and screen system so that they could watch movies in their own homes. Businessmen started showing films in community theaters. This created a legal problem for Edison.

Patents and Production Concerns

People were copying parts of Edison's designs to make cameras and projectors, and Edison believed they were doing so illegally. On October 24, 1907, Judge Christian Kohlsaat of the U.S. Court in Chicago agreed with Edison. He ruled that a William Selig had infringed on an Edison patent.

Another problem was Edison's first movie studio, the Black Maria. It had worked adequately for his initial movies, but it soon became necessary to find a larger building. In 1907 Edison opened the Thomas A. Edison, Inc. movie studio in the

Short films were made in Edison's Black Maria for more than ten years. In 1907, Edison built a larger and better studio for production in the Bronx, New York.

Bronx, New York. This one cost a bit more than the Black Maria: $100,000. Soon he and other moviemakers were producing movies that captured the interest of people across the country and around the world.

A Growing Industry

With several companies now producing movies and greater numbers of people wanting to see them, the industry rapidly grew in many directions. For example, by 1903 the Edison Company and Dickson's American Biograph Company had registered 350 films for copyright protection. As mentioned in chapter 2, the majority of these films were actualities, which meant they showed actual events.

Early in the 1900s these movies were often shown in theaters called nickelodeons that also promoted live comedians and singers. These entertainers, known as **vaudeville** players, would sometimes act out humorous skits, which were eventually put on film and became the basis for the first fictional movies such as romances, comedies, and dramas.

During this exciting time of motion-picture history, many people started going to the movies every weekend to watch the latest dramas that directors such as D. W. Griffith and Edwin S. Porter produced. The fictional films were so widely accepted that actuality movies became part of moviemaking history. In 1927 talking movies were introduced, and they became very popular.

VAUDEVILLE

Vaudeville shows first appeared in America in the 1880s. They were put on in communities that had a theater with a stage. Musicians played for the singers, and they even added sound effects to jokes or to dramatic skits acted out by the actors. Dancers and jugglers also entertained on vaudeville stages everywhere.

The word "vaudeville" comes either from *Vau de Vire*, which is a valley in France where many fifteenth-century songs originated, or from *voix de ville*, which is French for "street songs."

When movies started showing more and more of the acts normally seen on the vaudeville stages, the demand for this type of live entertainment declined. Some of the players and musicians were able to keep their careers by appearing in films, but others had to retire or find new lines of work.

The Jazz Singer was Hollywood's first feature film to include sound. The film industry would drastically change from producing silent films to making "talkies."

The Big Studios

Although the first actors and movie studios were on the East Coast, most American movies today are made in Hollywood, a district of Los Angeles, California. One of the main reasons directors and production companies moved west was to avoid legal problems while competing with Edison. Because the mail system took so long and because lawsuit papers had to be given in person, it was much harder for Edison to **sue** any of the people who tried to copy his machines after they had moved to California.

Another practical point in moving to California involved the warm air and consistently good weather. The great sunshine also offered much better lighting for films. By the 1920s the movie business had found a happy new home in California. The big studios included Paramount Pictures, Universal, and Metro-Goldwyn-Mayer (MGM). Sam Goldwyn was a major

MGM was the most powerful studio in its heyday. It was known for its high-powered stars and glossy, Technicolor films such as The Wizard of Oz *and* Gone with the Wind.

producer who hired quality directors, writers, and actors from the plays being produced in New York.

These writers and directors were the first to help actors and other workers on a movie set. They formed unions, groups that wielded power against big studios that tried to keep the pay low and the working hours long. When actors and writers stood together as a group, they had more strength to trade their services for fair wages and improved working conditions.

Newsreels and Serials

In place of actuality films came **newsreels**, which were films about news items that lasted about ten minutes. Now people who a few years earlier could only read about politics and cultures in other parts of the world could see the latest happenings each week! News from Europe and other continents came to the street corners of small-town America and changed the way Americans learned about faraway places. Scenes of soldiers fighting real battles and the latest inventions demonstrated by Thomas Edison himself were among the news stories that filled the big screens.

Some theater operators showed newsreels before a full-length movie. Others showed them during an intermission between two short **serials**. Serials were continuous stories that had the same characters in them in developing plots, shown in "chapters," with each episode usually ending in an exciting or dangerous scene. Most youngsters loved series featuring heroes such as

NEWS ON THE BIG SCREEN

Newsreels were filmed around the world and shown in neighborhood theaters during the 1920s–1940s. Some companies that made and distributed newsreels at the time were Fox Movietone, News of the Day, Paramount, and Universal.

Newsreels enabled Americans to learn more about their own politicians. People who had never seen a president in person could now watch and hear their leader. They could listen to new candidates and choose their elected officials more wisely than they could by listening to the radio or reading about them in newspapers. This photo shows former president Franklin Delano Roosevelt being filmed for a newsreel.

Superman, the Lone Ranger, and Zorro. These short fiction films became very popular and brought back viewers week after week to see what would happen next to their favorite characters.

All these new films and newsreels brought the need for good actors, good writers, and good camera operators into the motion-picture industry.

Growing Popularity Brings Changes

As the quality of movies improved, the quantity of movie-goers increased. During the Depression years in the 1930s and the World War II years of the early 1940s, movies helped people keep their minds off their troubles. One statistic estimates that more than 85,000 people visited movie theaters each week. Some story lines showed hungry and poor families barely hanging on to their farms but still thankful to have each other. Others showed just the opposite,

Crowds flock to the 1932 opening night of the movie Grand Hotel *in New York City's Time Square.*

with characters enjoying rich lifestyles. Both types of films gave people a sense of escape and relief from their everyday worries and hope for better times ahead.

Going to the movies changed too. Theaters that needed to be small enough for live actors to be seen and heard now had hundreds of seats and huge white screens that made actors' faces appear bigger than life. One of the most famous theaters is Grauman's Chinese Theatre. Opened in 1927 by Sid Grauman, the theater can seat more than two thousand people. It is still located on Hollywood Boulevard in Los Angeles and has become a major tourist stop. A main attraction is the theater's cement walkway, which has footprints and handprints of many movie stars.

Sid Grauman's dream came true when he built this theater and filled it with art from China. The jade-colored bronze roof rises 90 feet into the air and casts a dramatic effect when lit at night.

People loved watching the movies evolve from silent to talking, and from black-and-white to color. Another major change in motion pictures brought a lot more stars into the public's view and a lot more people in front of a smaller screen—the one known as the televison set.

NEW TECHNOLOGY

Motion-picture technology continued to grow throughout the twentieth century. Much of its growth came about because of a new form of entertainment on a small screen. During the 1920s, Philo Farnsworth invented a process of scanning images using electronic technology. His early work in electronic image transmission is what led to modern-day television (TV). By the late 1950s TV sets were part of American life. However, many people involved in the motion-picture industry were afraid that television might be a threat to motion-picture popularity.

Content Changes

People involved in the motion-picture industry worried that if families could watch quality programs for free on screens in their own homes, they wouldn't choose to spend money

Technology has provided us with new ways of viewing images. The television brings entertainment and news into our homes every day.

going to a theater. This concern helped bring about the wide-screen motion-picture technology. The thought was that if people showed an interest in a bigger picture, the motion-picture industry could survive television's popularity. Wide-screen technology was known as Cinemascope. It allowed the viewer to see a larger quantity of an image at one time. Cinemascope was first shown in 1953, and moviegoers loved the wide picture it offered. Almost immediately movie studios updated their cameras and equipment to make the wide-screen images people were willing to pay to see.

TV'S EARLY YEARS

The idea for television began when fourteen-year-old Philo Farnsworth wondered if an electron beam could scan an image one line at a time the same way he plowed his family's potato field. He figured that if he could invent a camera that could scan an image and then electronically reproduce it into a receiver, people far away from that image could instantly see its copy.

By the time he was twenty-one, he had found investors to back his idea. He began building sample electronic cameras and receivers with a tube he called an *Image Dissector*. He filed a patent in 1927 but did not invent a workable camera tube until 1933. He wanted to manufacture television sets but became involved in a legal battle.

The next few years were spent in court because the Radio Corporation of America (RCA) argued that Vladimir Zworykin, an engineer working for it, had invented television. Farnsworth eventually won the suit but still couldn't build sets, as all television production was halted when World War II began. This is why most people did not learn of television until the 1950s.

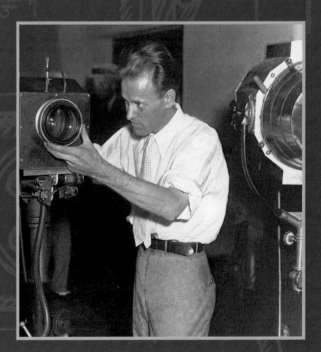

Another trend in the 1950s involved 3-D (three-dimensional) technology. Because our eyes are about 2.5 inches apart, they see two slightly different images. When those images are manipulated with 3-D glasses and 3-D projection equipment, people can see a greater depth in images. Moviemakers hoped that the films would seem more lifelike, which might draw more people into the movies. Unfortunately the red and green lenses in the glasses often distorted the color of the films. To make matters worse, the projection equipment could not always be fine-tuned in each theater, which caused

In the early 1950s, 3-D movies were the latest fad. Moviegoers viewed the film through special glasses that made the images seem to jump out of the screen.

the images to look blurry. These problems gave many movie-goers headaches and brought a quick end to 3-D movies.

In the 1980s another threat hit the movie industry: video-cassette technology. Now people could watch videos they'd recorded themselves with hand-held video cameras, using videocassette player machines connected to their TV sets. The motion-picture industry started selling videos of their movies to rental stores and retailers. Soon people across the world were standing in lines to rent or buy their favorite motion pictures to watch again and again. And to the movie

With the advancement of new technology, people gained the choice of watching a movie in a theater or at home using VCRs and videocassettes.

industry's surprise and relief, people kept showing up in movie theaters to watch new movies.

By the late 1990s digital technology had also fine-tuned depth perception imagery, improving the distorted images involved with 3-D. Soon 3-D images came to crisp, believable life in animated movies. Documentaries featuring wildlife and nature studies became popular when viewed in curved-screen theaters that were often housed in city museums. The curved screens enhanced the 3-D effect. When these films were first shown, people were amazed at the realistic quality, saying, "It looked as if you could step right into that world."

Celluloid Film Use Decreases

Perhaps the most important change in the motion-picture industry toward the end of the twentieth century was the decline in the use of celluloid film. Images could now be scanned electronically and recorded for future viewing on computer screens. Because of this, the need for buying, loading, and editing traditional celluloid took a backseat to digital photography in the motion-picture industry.

It's hard to predict at this point how this digital technology will affect the future of celluloid-film manufacturers. Many of the original camera and film companies have already adapted their product lines to sell digital cameras and accessories.

Electronic technology mixed with digital imaging brought forth the digital video age and DVD players. Retailers and

DVD players are rapidly replacing VCRs as viewers' choices increase with new motion-picture viewing inventions.

rental stores had to redesign their shelving to make room for compact discs that contained digital movies.

A Broader, More Educated View

One positive aspect of film and TV advancements was the educational element brought to viewers. Many students saw films in classrooms that showed historical or scientific information, which made the subject more interesting to some students. Another advancement in motion pictures was the use of satellite TV, which beams images from anywhere in the world into anyone's home in an instant.

During this amazing journey, as the motion picture emerged and changed, people around the world became more aware of each other than anyone could have imagined.

MOTION PICTURES: A TIMELINE

"Persistence of vision" defined by Peter Roget.
p. 43

Eadweard Muybridge uses sequential photography to show "motion."
p. 45

Thomas Edison meets Muybridge, begins work on the motion-picture camera and projector.
p. 45

Auguste and Louis Lumière patented the Cinématographe.
p. 22

Edison builds the Black Maria film studio.
pp. 25–26

| 1824 | 1834 | 1878 | 1884 | 1888 | 1891 | 1893 | 1897 |

Zoetropes are introduced.
p. 13

George Eastman patents a celluloid film.
p. 16

Edison's Kinetograph camera and Kinetoscope projector patents are filed.
p. 47

Edison begins legal battles over other movie inventions.
p. 54

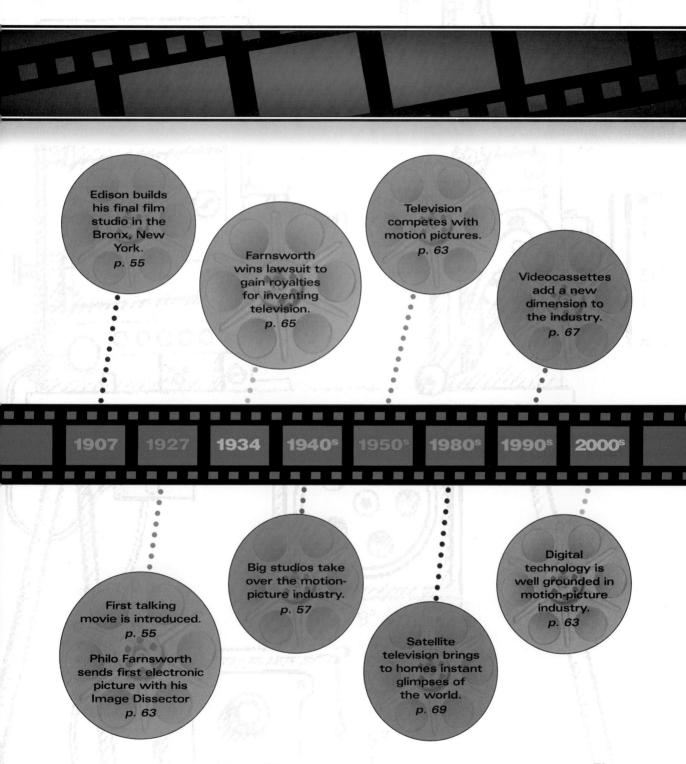

Edison builds his final film studio in the Bronx, New York.
p. 55

Farnsworth wins lawsuit to gain royalties for inventing television.
p. 65

Television competes with motion pictures.
p. 63

Videocassettes add a new dimension to the industry.
p. 67

1907 1927 1934 1940s 1950s 1980s 1990s 2000s

First talking movie is introduced.
p. 55

Philo Farnsworth sends first electronic picture with his Image Dissector
p. 63

Big studios take over the motion-picture industry.
p. 57

Satellite television brings to homes instant glimpses of the world.
p. 69

Digital technology is well grounded in motion-picture industry.
p. 63

GLOSSARY

apprentice: A person learning a skill under the supervision of an experienced worker

duplex telegraph: A telegraph that sends two messages at a time

emulsion: A mixture of liquid chemicals

film: A strong yet bendable celluloid substance, coated with an emulsion, for recording images

Image Dissector: A tube that electronically converts an image onto a screen

Insulators: Glass objects that prevent electrical currents from burning nearby materials

Kinetograph: One of the first motion-picture cameras

Kinetophone: The first machine to connect sound with moving pictures

Kinetoscope: The first motion-picture projector

magic lantern: A device used from the 1600s through the 1800s to project pictures

newsreels: Short news films first shown in the 1920s in movie theaters

patented: Recognized by the government as being invented or discovered by a particular person, who gains special rights to the product

projector: A device that enlarges an image and projects it onto a screen

sequential photography: Pictures taken in an orderly sequence or series so that when viewed, the image seems to be moving

serials: Short, fictional films with recurring characters, shown in movie theaters

studios: Buildings where movies or television shows are made *sue:* To file a lawsuit in court against someone

surveillance camera: A device in a home, a business, or a police car that records activity

telegraph system: A system that transmits messages by electric impulses through wires

vaudeville: Variety programs featuring live singers, dancers, and other entertainers

zoetrope: A round device with pictures on glass inside a rotating drum

zoopraxiscope: A device with photographs on a rotating glass disk that could be projected onto a screen

TO FIND OUT MORE

Books

Anderson, Kelly. *Thomas Edison*. San Diego, CA: Lucent Books, 1994.

Mitchell, Barbara. *Click! A Story About George Eastman*. Minneapolis, MN: Carolrhoda Books, 1986.

Thurman, Judith. *The Magic Lantern*. New York, NY: Atheneum, 1978.

Wood, Richard. *Great Inventions*. Alexandria, VA: Time Life Books, 1995.

Web Sites

Thomas Alva Edison
www.imahero.com/herohistory/alva_herohistory.htm
Biographical information on the inventor.

Devices of Wonder

www.getty.edu/art/exhibitions/devices/choice.html
An interesting cyber "exhibit" that features optical devices from before the invention of motion pictures.

The History of the Motion Picture

www.inventors.about.com/library/inventors/
   blmotionpictures.htm
A comprehensive guide to the history of motion pictures that includes links to related topics.

Organizations

American Film Institute
2121 North Western Avenue
Los Angeles, CA 90027
(323) 856-7600

Motion Picture Association of America
15503 Ventura Boulevard
Encino, CA 91436
(818) 995-6600

INDEX

ABOUT THE AUTHOR

I loved writing this book because when I was a kid my dad was a theater manager, so I spent lots of time playing hide and seek in theaters. For this book, I checked out books and video-tapes from our library about motion-picture history and Thomas Edison. I also visited Web sites with facts about motion pic-tures and anyone involved with the invention of them. You can learn anything you want if you are willing to read.

When I'm not writing, I help other writers make their words better. This gives me a chance to travel around the United States and meet lots of interesting peo-ple, especially students! This is my first book for Franklin Watts.